Blackbeard's Ship

Contents

Mick Gowar

Character illustrations by Jon Stuart

OXFORD

All aboard!

Welcome to the *Queen Anne's Revenge*. This ship belonged to the famous pirate Blackbeard. Come aboard and we'll show you around!

3

Blackbeard

Blackbeard and his pirate crew attacked ships in the Caribbean Sea 300 years ago. Blackbeard was very tall and VERY scary!

Today, when people think about pirates, they often think of pirates like Blackbeard.

Blackbeard often wore a tricorn hat and a crimson coat.

There are lots of stories told about Blackbeard. This makes it difficult to tell what is fact and what is fiction. This is what we *think* we know about Blackbeard ...

What was Blackbeard's real name?	Edward Teach
When and where was he born?	In Bristol, England, in about 1680
When and where did he die?	He was captured and killed by Captain Robert Maynard on 22nd November, 1718, in North Carolina, America.
How long was he a pirate for?	Only 2 years
How many ships did he raid?	At least 50 ships

What made Blackbeard so scary? His black beard, of course!

Privateers and pirates

In the time of Blackbeard, many wars were fought over who ruled the seas. When a country went to war, the **navy** was sent to fight. If there weren't enough ships in the navy, private ships called privateers were sent to attack the enemy.

When a privateer captured an enemy ship the captain was given a reward. He was also allowed to keep any goods stolen from the ship. Blackbeard's first ship was a privateer.

What a great ship!

When the wars ended, sailors who had fought on the privateers had to find other work. Many of them stayed at sea. They carried on attacking ships and stealing their **cargoes**. Like Blackbeard, they became PIRATES!

The Queen Anne's Revenge

Buried treasure

All pirates had one thing in common – they wanted treasure!

Pirate treasure could be gold, silver and jewels. Or it could be sugar, spices and cotton. Pirates also took things such as food and drink, weapons, tools, medicines and spare parts for their ship.

Pirates would divide the **booty** among themselves. The captain would get the biggest share.

FACT

Coins were popular booty because they were easy to share. In many stories and films, pirates have treasure chests full of *pieces of eight*. These were silver coins made in Spain and Mexico.

I wonder if Blackbeard buried his treasure?

There are lots of stories about pirates burying their treasure and drawing a map to help them find it again. But no one knows if this really happened or not. What do you think?

9

Lookout

The best place to spot an enemy ship was from the crow's nest high up at the top of the main mast. On a clear day, a **lookout** could spot a ship from a long way off. It was a dangerous job because there was a chance you could fall – especially if there was a storm.

Ship ho!

crow's nest

main mast

sail

A lookout would know who another ship belonged to by the colour or pattern on the flag.

Pirate flags were usually black with pictures of skulls on them.

Other sailors were scared of pirates. They often gave up without a fight when they saw a pirate flag.

Up on deck

Stories make a pirate's life sound exciting. But real life as a pirate was very hard. Most pirates were hungry, sick and poor.

Pirates could be at sea for weeks, looking for ships to raid. If they had no ships to attack pirates got bored. Sometimes they had fights. It was the captain's job to keep his crew under control.

I bet Blackbeard could keep his crew under control!

The Pirate Code

The Pirate Code was a list of rules that every person on board had to respect or else there would be trouble!

The worst crime was for a pirate to cheat his shipmates. If he was caught, he would face a nasty punishment. He could be made to walk the plank.

In stories and films, many pirates die fighting. Most real pirates died from hunger or disease. One disease that killed a lot of pirates was *scurvy*. Scurvy is caused by poor diet.

Shipshape

Pirates spent a lot of time looking after their ship.
Wooden sailing ships got very wet and dirty.
It was important to keep them clean to stop
accidents and to stop diseases spreading. The
decks had to be scrubbed every day.

Phew! Being a pirate was hard work!

Pirate ships were often damaged by rough seas and strong winds. Pirates had to patch the sails, mend the masts and make new ropes.

Even when they weren't at sea, pirates had to look after their ship. When they were in **port**, they would spend time scraping **barnacles** off the ship. Barnacles slowed the ship down.

Below deck

There were 300 pirates on board the *Queen Anne's Revenge*. They ate, slept and worked below deck. It was dirty and cramped and most of all … wet! The **hull** of the ship would leak and let in the sea water.

An artist's drawing of life as a pirate below deck.

Pirates spent a lot of time trying to stop leaks. They would seal the gaps between wooden boards with rope fibres. Then they would pour hot **pitch** on to the rope to make it waterproof.

Most pirates had only one set of clothes. They wore these every day! Being a pirate was dirty work but pirates hardly ever washed.

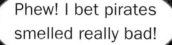

Phew! I bet pirates smelled really bad!

In the hold

Food, drink and other supplies were kept in the **hold** at the bottom of the boat. Heavy goods were stored in the middle to help balance the ship.

Rats were a real problem. They ate the food and spread disease.

After a few weeks at sea, there was usually no fresh food or water left. The cook had to use lots of spices to hide the taste of each rotten meal. Food would often be infested with **maggots**.

That rat looks hungry!

Time out

When they were not working, pirates liked to play games with cards and dice. Some liked to carve model ships from blocks of wood.

Pirates also liked to sing and dance. Many pirate ships had musicians on board.

Shanties were songs sung by sailors when they were doing hard or boring jobs. There were different shanties for different jobs.

Short or 'drag' shanties were sung when a job needed to be done quickly, like pulling ropes.

Halyard shanties were sung during heavy work, like hoisting the sails.

Capstan shanties were sung during long tasks, like lowering the anchor.

Turn over to find Cat and Tiger's very own sea shanty!

Cat and Tiger's sea shanty

A good strong wind to blow us west
To the Caribbean where the treasure is best.
Gold and silver, pieces of eight –
So haul the sails
The tide won't wait.

A pirate's life is the one for me –
Beneath the Jolly Roger on the rolling sea!

A strong south wind to Montego Bay
To hide our loot then sail away.
We've got a map, so never fear
We'll dig up the treasure when the coast is clear!

A pirate's life is the one for me –
Beneath the Jolly Roger on the rolling sea!

A strong north wind is what we need
To fill our sails and give us speed.
A navy ship is on our tail,
So haul away and hoist that sail!

A pirate's life is the one for me –
Beneath the Jolly Roger on the rolling sea!

A good west wind, to blow us home –
To port we'll sail, no more we'll roam.
We'll bid farewell to the Spanish Main
And steer a course for
    home again!

A pirate's life was the
    one for me –
But I've had enough of
    the rolling sea!

Glossary

barnacle — a small sea creature with a hard shell that fixes itself to the bottom of a boat

booty — stolen treasure

cargo — the goods carried by a ship from one place to another

hold — storage space in the bottom of a ship

hull — the bottom and sides of a ship

lookout — someone posted to keep watch for other ships or signs of land

maggot — a tiny worm that comes from an egg laid by a fly

navy — the ships and sailors who help protect a country

port — 1) a seaport 2) the left side of the ship (when you are facing front)

pitch — a sticky black substance made from tar

Index